CATCHING RAYS
An Activity Book About Light and Color

Written by **Dancy Burns**
Illustrated by **Rebecca Thornburgh**

SCHOLASTIC INC.
New York   Toronto   London   Auckland   Sydney

You can check your answers to all the puzzles in this book on pages 31 and 32. You can also color all of the pictures.

ISBN 0-590-76203-6

12 11 10 9 8 7 6 5 4 3   8 9/9 0 1 2/0

Printed in the U.S.A.
First Scholastic printing, August 1997

Over the Rainbow

When was the last time you saw a rainbow? Usually you see them when the sun comes out just after it rains. That's because sunlight streams through tiny raindrops still hanging in the air. The water drops separate sunlight into all of its parts—the colors of the rainbow!

Color in the rainbow below with the colors marked.

Can you imagine a world without color? The grass wouldn't turn green in the spring. The leaves wouldn't turn yellow and red in the fall. Flowers, animals, and the sky would all be shades of gray.
Hurray for color!

Match each picture on the left with its color on the right.

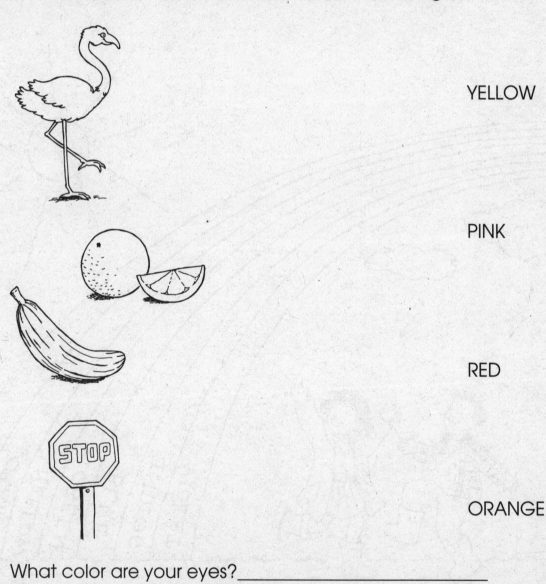

YELLOW

PINK

RED

ORANGE

What color are your eyes?_____

What is your favorite color? _____

Sunlight is "white" light. That means it doesn't **look** like any color, but it is actually made up of **all** colors. The moon reflects white light from the sun. Candles also give off white light. People have learned how to make white light without the sun or candles.

To find out what we need to make light, start at the arrow and write every other letter on the blanks below.

___ ___ ___ ___ ___ ___ ___ ___ ___ ___ ___

In 1879, Thomas Alva Edison invented the electric lightbulb. He used electricity to heat up a thin wire inside the bulb to make it glow.

Use the code to find out the name of the wire inside a lightbulb.

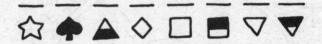

Thomas Edison invented more than 1,000 things, including the record player and the movie projector!

Wow, That's Fast!

Light travels roughly 186,000 miles in one second. It takes about 8 minutes for sunlight to reach Earth. The next closest thing in space that gives off light is a star called Proxima Centauri. Proxima Centauri and other stars are still so far away that we use a giant unit of measure to talk about the distance. One of these units equals the distance light travels through space in one year.

To find out the name of the special unit of measure, unscramble these letters and put the correct words in the blanks below.

IHGTL   EYARS

Proxima Centauri is 4.3 __ __ __ __ __ - __ __ __ __ __ away. It takes 4.3 years for its light to reach Earth.

Bonus Fact: Although Proxima Centauri is the closest star to Earth (except for the sun), it is not the brightest star we see. That's because other stars are larger and give off more light.

Prism Magic!

Raindrops can split white light into the colors of the rainbow, but so can certain triangular pieces of glass or plastic called **prisms**. When light enters a prism, it splits into its parts. A rainbow of color shines through another side of the prism.

PICNIC AREA

Circle the word PRISM 8 times in this picture.

I See the Light!

Light is energy, but the light we see is only a part of a much larger band of energy called the **electromagnetic spectrum**. The part of this larger band of energy that we can see is called **visible light**.

To find out another name for visible light, fill in each blank below with the letter that comes before it in the alphabet.

Look at the drawing on page 11. Do you recognize any of the other kinds of energy? What are they used for?

‾ ‾ ‾ ‾ ‾ ‾ ‾   ‾ ‾ ‾ ‾ ‾ ‾ ‾

W J T J C M F   T Q F D U S V N

ELECTROMAGNETIC SPECTRUM

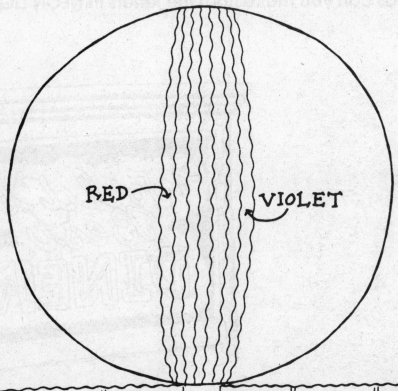

RED → VIOLET

| radio waves | micro-waves | infrared rays | | ultra-violet rays | X rays | gamma rays | cosmic rays |

ENERGY DECREASES   ENERGY INCREASES

Neon lights like the ones you see in store windows are actually tubes filled with neon gas. Neon gas has an orange color and the tubes have lights inside that make the gas glow. The glowing lights are so bright they catch people's attention.

How many words can you make from the letters in NEON LIGHTS?

Why Is the Sky Blue?

When white light reaches a colored object, the object absorbs almost all the colors in the light. Only light that is the color of the object bounces off and enters our eyes. That's why we see objects as the colors they are.

There are particles in the sky that absorb most of the sun's colors, but they reflect blue light most strongly. That's why the sky is blue.

The objects below are absorbing all the colors except red. Connect the dots to see what they are.

What are they? _____

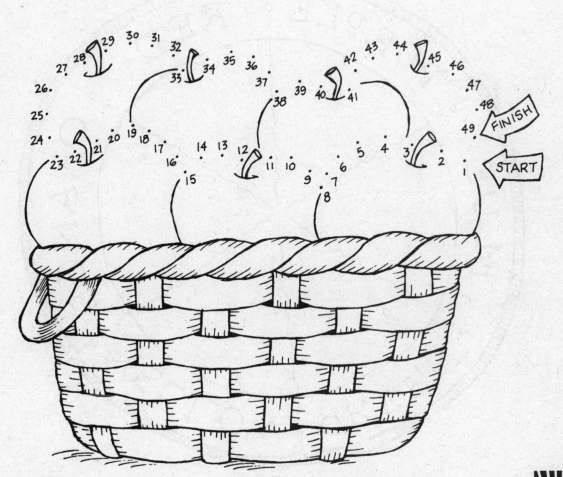

Did you know there are only **three** real colors and that all the other colors are **combinations** of those colors? It's true! The three "real" colors are called **primary colors** and they are red, yellow, and blue.

Color in the sections on this color wheel as they are marked. Can you figure out which primary colors combine to make the other colors?

What 2 colors make orange when mixed? _____ and _____

What 2 colors make green when mixed? _____ and _____

What 2 colors make purple when mixed? _____ and _____

What color do you get if you mix all the colors together? _____
Hint: Think about what happens when you paint.

If you mix red and yellow you get orange. If you add blue to the mixture, you get a color called "puce" (pyohs). It's a dark red. Try it!

Lots of color mixtures have interesting names. Follow the squiggly lines from each color name on the right to its description on the left.

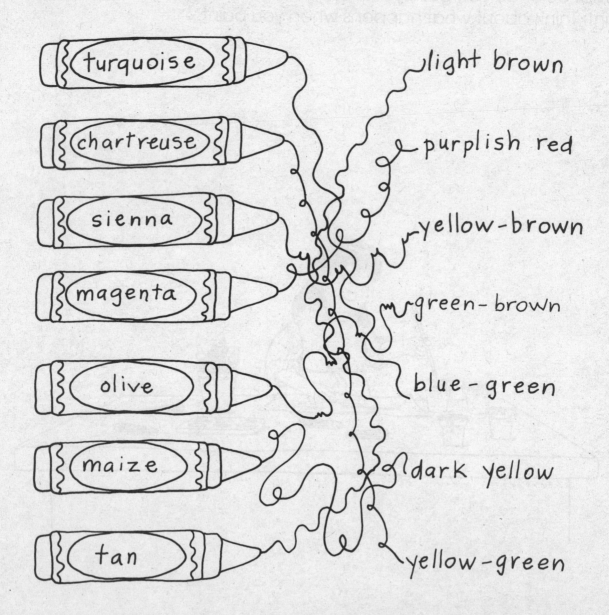

turquoise

chartreuse

sienna

magenta

olive

maize

tan

light brown

purplish red

yellow-brown

green-brown

blue-green

dark yellow

yellow-green

Can you find crayons, paints, or markers that are these colors?

Draw a picture with these new colors on this page.

Did you know that adding white to a mixture makes a color lighter and adding black makes a color darker? Did you know that adding gray makes bright colors look softer?

Experiment in your drawing on this page to see what happens.

Can Light Bend?

Light travels in a straight line, unless it hits a mirror or a prism that makes it take a turn. Light will also bend when it passes from one kind of material to another. For example, when light shines into a glass of water, it travels from the air into the glass and back into the air. The different materials make the light slow down and bend, often making objects in the water look bent or broken.

To find out the word for the kind of bending light does, write the first 2 letters of each word on the lines below.

RED FRESH ACHE TINY ONION

— — — — — — — — — —

Bonus question: What happens when you look at yourself in a still lake or pond?

Light Up My Life

Light is important to our day. Think about what it would be like if it were light at night when you go to sleep and dark during the day when you go to school.

Study this picture carefully. Circle the things that give off light. Then take the memory test on page 22.

Circle the correct answers to the questions below. See if you can remember without looking back at pages 20-21.

1. What kind of pet does the boy in the bedroom have?

   Cat   Dog   Lizard

2. How many books are on the boy's desk?

   Three   Six   Four

3. From what you saw in the boy's bedroom, what is his favorite sport?

   Basketball   Soccer   Baseball

4. Which of the following is the title of one of the books on the desk?

   All About Math   *All About History*   *All About Science*

5. What shape is the light on the boy's ceiling?

   Circle   Triangle   Square

6. What is the boy reading?

   Captain Crash comic book   *I Love Dogs* book   a letter

7. What is the boy eating?

   Popcorn   Candy bar   Apple

8. What time is it in the picture?

   Noon   4 o'clock   8 o'clock

Hot Stuff!

The sun is millions of miles away yet it still gives us enough light and heat for the whole planet. Heat is produced deep inside the sun when a gas called hydrogen turns into a different gas called helium. Heat and light are released during this change. So on a really hot summer day, what's really happening is that lots of hydrogen is being turned into lots of helium inside the sun.

To find out what this process of changing hydrogen into helium is called, write the letters in number order.

Code:

6 = N
4 = I
1 = F
3 = S
2 = U
5 = O

___ ___ ___ ___ ___

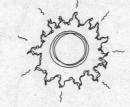

Never look directly at the sun. It's so hot, it can burn your eyes! The sun can burn your skin, too, so remember to wear sunglasses **and** sunscreen outside.

For a lightbulb to work, electricity must flow in a complete circle called a **circuit**. The electricity travels from a big generator somewhere in your town or city through wires to your house and then to the lightbulb, which lights up. The electricity continues to flow back in a circle to the generator. As long as the electricity flows in a circle, the light stays on. When you turn the switch off, you break the circuit and the lightbulb turns off.

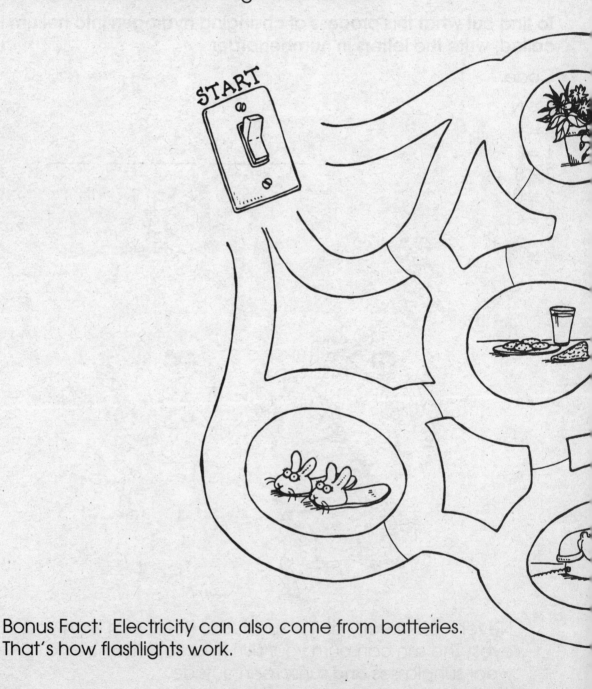

START

Bonus Fact: Electricity can also come from batteries. That's how flashlights work.

Draw a line through the maze below to show how the electricity flows through the wires from the light switch to the lightbulb.

FINISH

The Eyes Have It!

When you look at an object, such as an ice cream cone, **light** rays reflected off the object pass into your **eye** through the **pupil**. The rays go through a **lens** and then strike the **retina** at the back of your eye. The ice cream cone on the retina is upside down. The **optic nerve** sends a message about the ice cream cone to your **brain** and your brain turns the image right side up. Yum! Yum!

Circle these words in the puzzle below.

light   eye   pupil   lens   retina   optic nerve   brain

P A B T G J I I K O
N U M H L A H J N S
P O P G F K L B M N
O P T I C N E R V E
E D C L L Q P A A L
P G S R R E T I N A
Q E T S D Y C N A D
U V R W X E C B Y Z

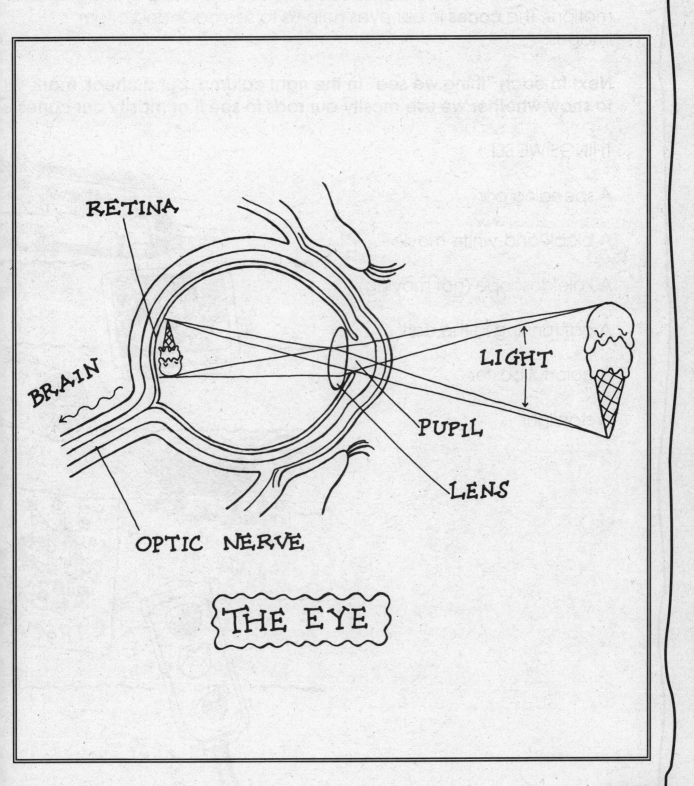

RETINA

BRAIN

OPTIC NERVE

LIGHT

PUPIL

LENS

THE EYE

Rods and Cones

The **rods** in our eyes help us to see black and white, dim images, and motion. The **cones** in our eyes help us to see color and bright images.

Next to each "thing we see" in the right column, put a check mark to show whether we use mostly our rods to see it or mostly our cones.

THINGS WE SEE

A speeding car

A black-and-white movie

A kaleidoscope (not moving)

A cat running in the dark

A colorful poster

A stoplight

Colorful Crosword

Use the clues to complete the puzzle below.

Across

1. Causes light to bend.
3. Red, yellow, and blue are _____ colors.
5. The sun and _____ give off light from space.

Down

2. _____ inside the sun releases heat and light.
4. Yellow and blue together make _____.
6. Neon lights have neon _____ in them.

Answers

Page 4

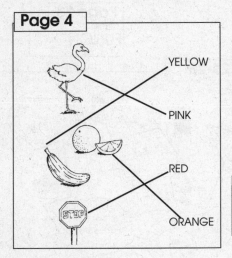

YELLOW

PINK

RED

ORANGE

Page 5

ELECTRICITY

Page 6

FILAMENT

Page 7

LIGHT-YEARS

Pages 8-9

Pages 10-11

VISIBLE SPECTRUM

Page 12

one tie sign lit stone
none gilt hit on lens
hot son

Page 13

Apples

Pages 14-15

red and yellow
blue and yellow
red and blue
brownish black

Pages 18-19

REFRACTION

Page 16

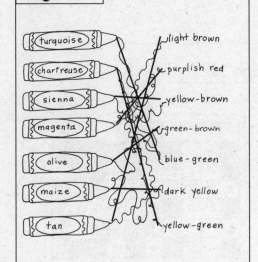

turquoise — light brown

chartreuse — purplish red

sienna — yellow-brown

magenta — green-brown

olive — blue-green

maize — dark yellow

tan — yellow-green

Pages 20-21

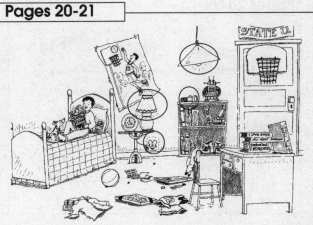

Answers

Page 22

1. What kind of pet does the boy in the bedroom have?

   Cat   (Dog)   Lizard

2. How many books are on the boy's desk?

   Three   Six   (Four)

3. From what you saw in the boy's bedroom, what is his favorite sport?

   (Basketball)   Soccer   Baseball

4. Which of the following is the title of one of the books on the desk?

   All About Math   All About History   (All About Science)

5. What shape is the light on the boy's ceiling?

   Circle   (Triangle)   Square

6. What is the boy reading?

   (Captain Crash comic book)   I Love Dogs book   a letter

7. What is the boy eating?

   Popcorn   Candy bar   (Apple)

8. What time is it in the picture?

   Noon   (4 o'clock)   8 o'clock

Page 23

FUSION

Pages 24-25

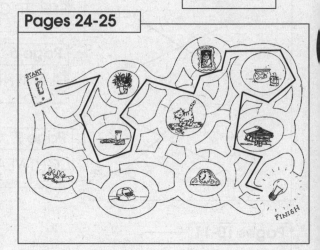

Pages 26-27

Pages 28-29

Page 30

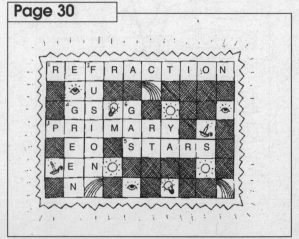